Is A Perfect Heart God's Design?

Experiencing His love
in its fullness
will inevitably lead to
A perfect heart

**Being confident of this very thing,
that He which hath begun a good work in you
will perform it until the day of Christ Jesus**
(Philippians 1:6)

Published by:
2018 Charlene Gray

No part of this book may be reproduced, stored in a retrieval system, or transmitted in any form, or by any means, electronic, mechanical, photocopying, recording or otherwise, without prior permission of the author.

Unless otherwise indicated, Scripture quotations are from the Holy Bible. Scripture quotation identified KJV are from the King James Version.

Table of Contents

Introduction   5

Chapter One
Exposed Heart   9

Chapter Two
A clean heart/ A Pure Heart   19

Chapter Three
A Forgiving Heart   25

Chapter Four
A Heart of Love   35

Chapter Five
The Perfect Heart   53

Acknowledgements

First, I would like to thank my husband for his support and tireless work in helping bring this book to completion. I am so thankful for my sons' support, encouragement and belief that I could do this. I thank Pastor, Rohan Peart for his insight and editing of the book. I wish to thank Minster, Elaster Nickelberry for his design of the book's cover. He captured what I had envisioned perfectly. I am thankful for the support and prayers of my Pastor, Gerald Vickers and the members of the Jonesboro, Church of God of prophecy. Most of all I would like to thank God for entrusting me with this work and giving me the grace and incentive to finish it.

Introduction

Is it possible to have a heart after God? What a question to ponder and roll around in the mind of human beings. The heart is the real person for from it flow the issues of life. In God's world the heart must be perfect and there are no exceptions. How then can this process of perfection be started and who can bring it about? Well! It starts by acknowledging that we need a heart change and admitting that the heart of mankind is bent on evil. That is, it goes after what is satisfactory to itself and brings pleasure even though it can bring about pain and lasting repercussions.

There is an inclination toward selfishness that is deeply seated in us as earthly creatures. From our early days we strive to get what we want and throw temper tandems if we don't get our way. We must be taught to share what we have with others, but that still does not completely rid us of our selfishness and the "me syndrome". I must admit that there are still some things that I have to say "no" to because it shows my selfish desire to have my own way, and my not having any concern for others who may be hurt or affected by it.

To learn to think of others as more deserving than ourselves takes a while to master. Yet, it can be done especially if we have a relationship with the Lord, Jesus the Son of the Highest God. When He is Lord in or over our lives then our hearts will begin to undergo changes. His Spirit in us is changing our selfish desires and motives. When He is at work in the deepest part of the heart anything that is hidden will be brought into the light.

We would like to think that we know our hearts and that we are not capable of doing anything corrupt or giving in to behavior that maybe other people give in to. This thinking is contrary to what our Creator says about the human heart. Yes, I like to think that I would never hurt anyone by saying mean and hateful things about them to someone else; and that I would never post something on social media about another person even though I could post it anonymously. I like to think that I am inwardly good and that I would never intentionally speak negatively about another person. We all tend to feel this way and please don't ask any of us to admit that this is not the case.

The reality is that we need a heart change, or we need a good heart surgeon who can go in with his surgical instrument and cut away at what is causing the heart to be unclean, evil and filled with darkness. There was a chorus that was popular among believers in the late nineties that simply stated, "Change my heart, O God, make it ever true; change my heart O God, may I be like you". If we are honest with ourselves this is still a song that should be the cry of our hearts. This is for those who name the name of Christ and are representing Him to this world by the way we live in transparency. It is the world that needs to see what has taken place in the life of the believer to give them a desire or thirst to want to find out more about God and how to become part of His family.

    The heart is the very center of our being and every one of us can experience a heart change if we are willing to allow the One who is able to change it; and make it completely new – recreated after His own heart which is perfect and holy. The one that can do this is God Himself and He can remove the heart that is black, filthy, sinful and totally corrupt; and make it clean and as pure as snow before Him. The outcome will be a perfect heart that is reborn and made new all over again. The heart that He is looking for and going after is one that looks just like His.

    There will be nothing in us that resembles sin, darkness, evil or death. All will be made new. We should all want this, but unfortunately everyone does not. However, those of us who really desire this, and are going after it with all that is within us; knows for certain that God wants this for us more than we want it for ourselves. Go for the perfect heart and let's learn about what we can possibly do to get there shall we!

Chapter One

Exposed Heart

Do you recall the day that you called out to Jesus to come and be Lord of your life; how you asked Him to make His home in your heart? I remember asking Him to come in to my heart and change my whole life. I told Him that my heart was His and that He could do with it what He chose to do. Did I mean what I said? Yes, I did, and I still do even though there are times when I allow my own will to crowd out His will in my heart.

How can I really know my heart? I think the first step to take is to consider the possibility that something has been deeply hidden away in your heart that you are not aware of. It can be a very slight tinge of resentment that we are feeling toward someone; or maybe a seed of bitterness is creeping in and trying to take root. Since we have made Jesus Lord over our hearts then He does have a right to reveal to us what He sees in it. There should be no feeling of animosity over His showing you or me what is displeasing to Him, and that is an impending threat to our intimacy with Him. Jesus' Spirit is very gentle and kind and wants what is best for all who are part of God's family. There is nothing hidden from His gaze so there is absolutely no way He can be fooled; and the best thing to do then is to come clean by getting it out in the open to be done with the root cause of the problem. If I want my heart to be completely pure before God, I must be honest and accept His revelation about what is really in me.

   Consider David, a man after God's own heart and even though he failed miserably on several occasions he never turned away from his relationship with God. God is the one that said this about him, "For I have found David the son of Jesse, a man after mine own heart; which shall fulfill all my will" (Acts 13:22 KJV). How can this possibly be true when we know that David broke two of the Ten Commandments; and yet God can say he is the man that is after my heart and does whatever is pleasing to Me?" Even though David grievously sinned against God; could it possibly be that he was so in sync with God's perfect heart that he never quit seeking God's mercy. David's heart was so injured by his sinful acts that his physical health began to deteriorate. While keeping his sin hidden (so he thought) for about a year or more, God was dealing with him to come clean. He did not yield to God's prompting, even though his heart was sensitive to God's Spirit of conviction. David got to the point where he could not sleep nor eat. He became a very miserable person. His heart was crying out to be exposed and healed. Could this possibly have been the time he asked God, "Search me, O God, and know my heart: try me, and know my thoughts: And see if there be any wicked way in me and lead me in the way everlasting" (Psalm 139:23-24, KJV)?

When the heart is sorrowful and broken because of a sinful act, it is at this point that a person is ripe for repentance (2 Corinthians 7:10). God was patiently waiting on David and He knew how broken he was at that moment. So, God gives David the mercy and help he needed. He sent the Prophet Nathan to share with him a story [allegory] of a rich man who had everything, and a poor man who had nothing except one little ewe lamb. The poor man had purchased this lamb and brought it home and raised it with his children. It was loved by all and allowed to eat and even drank from his cup; it was like a daughter to him.

As the story continues, a traveler comes to the rich man, and to avoid taking one of his own flock or herd to prepare for his guest, he took the poor man's lamb and prepared it instead. Now take notice how this story affected David. After hearing the story, his reaction was one of anger and in that anger, he gave his opinion to Nathan by saying, "As the LORD liveth, the man that hath done this thing shall surely die" (2 Samuel 12:5b,

KJV). David is livid, and his judgment is that the man should restore the lamb fourfold, because he had done this without pity. David was moved by his own emotions and made it clear that the man's actions were deserving of death. However, he decided that he would be lenient on him by requiring the restoration of about four times the value of the one lamb. His reasoning was that this man had done this without showing any pity or compassion toward the poor man.

Nathan's true purpose in confronting the king with this story was to remind David of the sin he had committed. He does not hesitate even though David is the king, since he feared God much more than he feared the king. "And Nathan said to David, Thou art the man. Thus, saith the LORD God of Israel, I anointed thee king over Israel, and I delivered thee out of the hand of Saul; And I gave thee thy master's house, and thy master's wives into thy bosom, and gave thee the house of Israel and of Judah; and if that had been too little, I would moreover have given unto thee such and such things. Wherefore hast thou despised the commandment of the LORD, to do evil in his sight? thou hast killed Uriah the Hittite with the sword, and hast taken his wife to be thy wife, and hast slain him with the sword of the children of Ammon" (2 Samuel 12:7-9, KJV).

Even though God had waited without passing judgment for a space of two years, David was still guilty before Him. Now! It is time for God to give His sentence for David's behavior against the Lord. This man, chosen and loved by God and living in an intimate relationship with God had failed. David had a choice before yielding to the dictates of the flesh. He could have resisted the replay of the image of Bathsheba running over and over in his mind. Had he resisted, God would have helped him stand strong against the temptation. Unfortunately, we allow ourselves to succumb to the lure of temptation. This is what happened in David's case.

God's Word will not be held in contempt. It does not matter if we are the most spiritual persons on earth and have been used to win many souls to God. If we began to take His Word lightly or even despise it, we are asking for His wrath. This is exactly what David did and he would suffer the consequence of his behavior. Because David had slain Uriah with the sword even though it was the sword of the Ammonites that killed Uriah, but the truth of the matter it was as though the sword was in the hand of David. God said, "Now therefore the sword shall never depart from thine house; because thou hast despised me, and hast taken the wife of Uriah the Hittite to be thy wife" (2 Samuel 12:10 KJV). To despise God's Word is to despise God, because His word is synonymous with Himself.

God is holy, and He hates sin and rebellion against His word. Though David was king he had to face up to what He had done. God could have rejected him and removed him from being king over Israel. Instead the

Lord said, "Thus saith the LORD, Behold, I will raise up evil against thee out of thine own house, and I will take thy wives before thine eyes, and give them unto thy neighbour, and he shall lie with thy wives in the sight of this sun. For thou didst it secretly: but I will do this thing before all Israel, and before the sun" (2 Samuel 12:11-12, KJV). Again, God is holy, and He will not be mocked or allow His word to be held in contempt. How can this possibly be the man whom God loves, holds in high esteem, and calls him the apple of His eye? This shows us that we are all fallible and need to pay attention to what may be going on in our hearts. If there is any inclination of lust for something or someone that does not belong to us, we should allow the Holy Spirit to bring it out in the open before it overpowers us and leads to action. When sin is conceived it leads to death.

As David stands before the prophet, he is filled with fear and he tell Nathan,"...I have sinned against the LORD" (2 Samuel 12:13, KJV). He is not sure whether he is going to live or die because of his sin. Nathan knows that he is afraid, and he tells him, "And Nathan said unto David, The LORD also hath put away thy sin; thou shalt not die" (2 Samuel 12:13, KJV). David's confession opens the door for God to forgive him and take his sin away. God knew about David's sins and allowed him to endure the burden of them until he was ready to admit what he had done. The moment came, and God sent His prophet with a word which would bring about total repentance; therefore, it would bring about cleansing and a restoration of the intimacy between he and God. When we harbor sinfulness in our hearts, God does not and will not hear our prayer. If there is any love affair between what we have done to the point that it is in our hearts and on our minds, then it becomes a wedge between the Lord and ourselves. Once we decide that we want to be free from whatever it is that is holding us in bondage then we are ready to take the next step. "If we confess our sins, He is faithful and just to forgive us of our sins; and to cleanse us from all unrighteousness" (1 John 1:9, KJV).

      The saga of David's behavior continues as he must endure God's severe punishment. Remember sin must be dealt with and so therefore David had to bear the consequences of what he had done. In behaving in this manner, he not only dishonored God, but he gave ammunition to the Lord's enemies to speak evil against God as well. Through Nathan, God tells David that the child he has conceived out of the adulterous relationship will most certainly die. As soon as the words came forth from the prophets' mouth David's little son was suddenly taken ill. This man was a lover of God, how could this have happened? David, who wrote that "he hated with perfect hatred those who did not honor God" and considered such people his enemies, since this was how God viewed them. In having succumbed to the lust of the eyes and the desires of the flesh he gives God's enemies a reason to criticize God in a jeering and disdainful way – It was as if David was guilty of speaking the words himself. We must remember that we represent Jesus to a world that scrutinizes and judges our actions to have an opportunity to dishonor or defame our God. I know that I have spent quite a bit of time on David and this dark time in his life, but it is a good reminder that we all must stay opened to God's Spirit and deny our flesh the opportunity to overpower us, causing us to yield to the cravings of sin.

      I believe the one thing King David counted on was that God's mercy endured forever. He appealed to that mercy by falling before God in prayer on behalf of his little son.   David not only prayed but he fasted and lay all night on the floor. He was possibly thinking "God you have shown me mercy, please do it again for my child." The older of his house servants came to him in the night and tried to lift him from the floor, but he would not get up, neither did he eat any food with them. This lasted for seven days and the Scripture states, "And it came to pass on the seventh day, that the child died" (2 Samuel 12:18a, KJV). His servants were afraid to tell him that he had died, for they feared that he may try to harm himself. They went back and forth, "should we tell him that the child is dead?" David knew that he was dead when he heard them whispering, "He asked is the child dead? And they said, He is dead" (2 Samuel 12:19b, KJV). The servants were afraid that David would commit suicide after hearing that his son had died. Satan wanted to do as much damage to this man as he possibly could.

God had ordained him to be shepherd over His people. Most importantly, God had decreed that through him and his descendants, the Messiah would ultimately come. Satan's strategy failed to work because David got up, washed, and changed clothes. What he does after that proves that he was genuinely sorry for his actions against God. Nor was he angry or bitter toward Him because of the child's death. David's heart is crying out for His God, so he goes to the House of the Lord and worshiped. Beloved, when we love God and our hearts are confident that we really love Him; and if or when we fail Him in any way we must keep running back to His presence. We must not allow condemnation to cause us to turn away from His mercy and grace. God will never give up on those who are His; He will chase after us and bring us back into fellowship with Him. So, then what should the cry of our hearts be? I believe that it should be the one that David's heart cried, "Search me, O God, and know my heart: try me, and know my thoughts: And see if there be any wicked way in me and lead me in the way everlasting" (Psalm 139:23-24, KJV).

Prayer: Lord, you are the One that can bring about a heart change. Give us the grace to be honest with ourselves and most importantly with You. It is impossible for any of us to deceive You, so help us to be real and transparent with no cover up. Thank you for your help Lord Jesus. Amen!

Chapter 2

A Clean Heart Equals a Pure Heart

Most of us are familiar with the old saying, "Cleanliness is next to Godliness". Could this be addressing the heart of a person rather than the outward condition? Possibly! I like things to look clean, feel clean and smell clean. Included in my list are: my house, laundry and my car. At one point I was obsessed with keeping things neat and as clean as possible. This was very challenging in that I had a full-time job, a husband, and three sons along with other outside activities. Eventually, after wearing myself out in trying to keep everything perfect it finally dawned on me that things just didn't have to be that way. So, after years of stressing and trying to be the "super homemaker," wife and mother I decided to do what was most necessary. I still like things to be in order and not chaotic, but it does not fill me with stress to the point that it has to be brought back into order immediately. However, there is a good feeling that comes when things are clean and smell nice and fresh. The opposite is true when things are dirty, and smelly. You feel depressed and engulfed by a cloud of gloomy darkness. If this is the case with our natural environment, what affect does uncleanliness have on our hearts? There are times when we just let things go and come to the point that we must act or else we will be overcome by the attack of the adversary against our hearts.

The heart or the inward person is what God communicates with – It is the real you. Without Jesus in our hearts we have no connection to God because we are spiritually dead. The heart that is not regenerated or re-created by Jesus' blood is sinful and filled with blackness. It is unclean and devoted to things that cannot bring about purity with no desire for change. A changed heart can never happen without the work of God's Spirit in a person's life. The Holy Spirit is the agent of God who can come and shine the light of life on the heart that is unclean, and dead because of sin. God created Adam, the first man with a pure nature………. as a matter of fact, he had God's heart. The truth of the matter is that the very glory of God lived in him. When he chose to disobey the command God had given him concerning eating of the "tree of knowledge of good and evil," his pure nature became filled with sin and immediately he was disconnected from the heart of God. Adam lost his clean and pure conscience and gained a heart filled with darkness. Therefore, all his descendants even those yet unborn were plunged into the same sinful nature.

God who is filled with a passionate desire for children was not going to allow his arch enemy, Satan to thwart His plan for all of mankind. He passed judgment on the serpent, man and the woman. When God sentenced the serpent he also passed sentence on the one who had devised the plan to entice the woman to disobey God, that old serpent known as the devil, Lucifer or Satan. In Genesis 3:15 we have the prophecy spoken from God's mouth concerning the defeat of Satan.

The One who would come, "The Seed" would be God in flesh to restore man back to God. As Bible believers we know the one who came was Jesus Christ the Son of God. He took on the form of a servant and lowered Himself even to the death on the cross. He was the Lamb that took the sins of the whole world upon Himself (John 1:31). Jesus took our place for us to partake of His righteousness. There was no sin in Him and therefore He as fully man and fully God could die on behalf of sinful man, and by doing so defeat sin in the flesh. This had to be done to clear the way for man to be born again and have a brand-new heart.

A clean heart is the prerequisite to opening the way for a pure heart. In the Gospel it is stated that Jesus was invited to dinner by a Pharisee, one of the religious groups of His day. This man became very bent out of shape after observing that Jesus did not wash His hands before dinner. Jesus did not say that it was not necessary to wash one's hands, but He let them know that they needed to pay more attention inwardly than outwardly. Listen to His words to them, "And the Lord said unto him, now do ye Pharisees make clean the outside of the cup and the platter; but your inward part is full of ravening and wickedness. Ye fools, did not he that made that which is without make that which is within also? But rather give alms of such things as ye have; and, behold, all things are clean unto you. But woe unto you, Pharisees! for ye tithe mint and rue and all manner of herbs, and pass over judgment and the love of God: these ought ye to have done, and not to leave the other undone" (Luke 11:39-42 KJV).

Maybe the Pharisee was thinking about what the Psalmist wrote in Psalm 24. The Psalmist had asked a question, "Who will ascend into the hills of the Lord" (Psalm 24:3a, KJV)? Then he gives a reply to that question, "He who has clean hands and a pure heart shall ascend into the hills" (Psalm 24:4a, KJV). Could he possibly considered clean hands more important because you can see dirty hand; but the heart you could not see, and no one could ever know what was really in the heart?

The main point for us to take away from this is that when all the junk within us from past wounds, failures, regrets, animosity, guilt and shame is cleared out; our hearts will be purified by the sprinkling of the blood of the Lamb; then will we find ourselves moving much closer to having a pure heart.

Natalie Grant, a Dove Award winning artist makes a simple but profound statement in her song entitled "Clean". She says, "There's nothing too dirty that You can't make worthy, You wash me in mercy I am clean." Again, this is true and made possible because of that precious blood of Jesus. This song can be downloaded via most music venues.

What is so important about the heart being pure? How about if we let Jesus answer that for us, "Blessed are the pure in heart for they shall see God" (Matthew 5:8, KJV). The Psalmist that penned Psalm 24:4 was spot on I would say.

Prayer: Lord you only can search our hearts and you alone know everything that is hidden there. Help us to lay it all open to you so that the light of your Word can shine through; and take away the dirt that may be there Lord. In your name Jesus let it be so. Amen!

Chapter 3

A Forgiven Heart

Is it easy to forgive someone who has hurt you? Maybe they physically harmed you, or verbally abused you, betrayed or lied to you. The answer is no! It is not easy to forgive. I know from experience that this is no easy task, mainly because it is in our human make up to want to hold on to grudges. In other words, it has to do with, "they did this to me, how could they?" Therefore, since this is the case, it gives every one of us the right to hold on to grudges so we choose the option of not letting them go. When this path is taken it does more damage to the individual holding the grudge than to the person that we choose not to forgive.

When we harbor unforgiveness in our hearts this can lead to both emotional issues as well as physical problems. There are several books that have been written on this subject today; some of them by medical professional and others by individuals like you and me. One may question why then should we work at forgiving those who have hurt us? The answer is that there are benefits available to us when we simply say to that person or persons "I forgive you". One such benefit is that we experience a release in our heart. The tightening and restriction that takes place in the heart which is brought on by stress and anger will be released when we let go of unforgiveness. It is amazing how just saying to someone "I choose to forgive you and will no longer react to you in anger, nor refuse to speak, or have any interaction with you" will liberate the inner person, cause the heart rate to become normal, and lower blood pressure. These are all positive results that can happen immediately once action is taken to forgive.

    There is something else to consider when dealing with forgiveness and un-forgiveness. For example, if there is a situation where you have caused someone pain by your words or actions and you know this to be true and you want to make it right. So, you have tried to resolve the problem and work things out with this individual by calling or messaging to say that you are genuinely sorry for your actions. You tell them that you are asking them to please forgive you. You do all that you can to convince them that you did not mean to cause emotional or physical harm; and at the time your actions were based on fear of what may happen. The decision that was made at that time is now the cause of the problem in the relationship. What else can be done when the other person is not willing to at least talk about the situation? They are not interested in getting together to try to resolve the problem that will at least open the way for possible forgiveness and reconciliation.

When there is no desire to discuss what happened on the part of the other individual, the only thing that you can do is to release them, since you have done what was required of you to resolve the problem. In this case whenever one person refuses to let the other off the hook they are the one who is being held in bondage by not being willing to forgive. We must remember when choosing to live and walk according to the Word of God we are only responsible for how we live our own lives. Once we have personally made the choice to do what is right, and begin to live as an example for others, we are now doing what God expects of us. However, we must understand that ultimately, they are responsible for living out their own convictions and beliefs. It is impractical for us to demand that a person do what is right. God will not force a person to do the right thing. He leaves it up to the individual to decide. He gives them the choice to obey or to disobey His instructions. Again, it is all about our choices.

Jesus taught His disciples about the need for forgiveness. He made it clear that unforgiveness was not an option. When we choose to forgive someone of their offenses against us we will experience forgiveness in return from the Father. Maybe this sounds unfair since what was done to us was real and we feel that the person responsible for causing us harm should be held accountable for their actions. We can view this from another angle. Maybe the person who asks for forgiveness is not at all sorry for his or her behavior. Maybe they are just going through the motion for the time being, but as soon as the situation has settled down they do the same thing or possibly worse than before.

     Again, we as believers are to follow the teaching of our Lord and Savior. It may be difficult to keep forgiving an individual repeatedly, especially when they are guilty of the same offense. This does not mean that we should stay in a situation that may cause physical harm to ourselves or the other person. If there is a real threat of this happening then it would be better to tell them that you forgive them, but you would prefer to keep your distance. This is using wisdom to avoid a confrontation that may not end well.

     There must be a willingness to forgive those who have hurt us. This is the first step that leads to forgiveness. Rehearsing or reliving everything that was done or said will not solve anything. It is true that maybe the person or persons involved does not deserve forgiveness, but this same truth can be applied to us. Forgiveness is not easy but when it is applied the outcome will outweigh the inward struggle. When forgiveness is given from the heart it causes a tremendous weight to be lifted and there is freedom because the burden is no longer being carried. Where there once was the need to limit communication with the person that had caused you hurt or pain, you find that you do not want to just avoid them as you did before, for you are not being gripped by anger or a need to express your feeling verbally anymore. This is what happens when we willingly choose to forgive. We are the ones that experience the freedom of letting go.

A forgiving heart is a heart that is concerned not just for itself but thinks about the welfare of others. We can attempt to justify our unforgiving attitude by using the excuse that we are only human. Therefore, we are not expected to allow people to take advantage of us especially if we can help it. We can also argue that God does not expect us to allow people to just walk all over us without defending our selves. Yet, even in the defense of our actions we should think about the possible consequences. It could be that we are confronted with someone who is very boisterous, demanding, disrespectful and inconsiderate. When our motives are called into question leaving no space for communication nor resolution of differences. Again, when it all comes down to it we must do what we feel is right regardless of the outcome which is all that is required of us. Sure, everybody would like to have their differences resolved never having to deal with them again. Unfortunately, we are not all wired the same. Sometimes people that are in our lives do not care about doing what is right. They would rather hold on to grudges than release them whereby setting themselves free.

Ultimately there is a greater benefit that can be gained once we are willing to forgive others. That benefit is that we are being obedient to what Jesus commanded us to do. He told Peter that it was not enough to forgive someone their trespasses only seven times, but that he was to forgive them seventy times seventy (See Matthew 18:22). Forgiveness then is not just a onetime act, but it is a process that takes time and effort. Jesus wanted him to understand that this is a continuous attitude of forgiveness regardless of how many times a person does wrong toward us. Is this really something that can be done? Yes, it is possible in that Jesus will help us and give us the ability to forgive. He is our example and when we commit to His teachings and ways of doing things He will give us more grace to carry out those things that we simply cannot do on our own.

The second thing to remember is that if we choose not to operate in forgiveness we will suffer the consequences. The result of our behavior is that we have closed the door on experiencing the forgiveness of God in our lives. God is the one that has provided each of us forgiveness through the Person of Jesus Christ. When we hold on to what we have experienced in the past, such as bitterness, anger, hurt feelings and the unjust treatment that we received from others, we are the ones taking the pill, which when taken every day for a period will be releasing a deadly poison within us. If allowed to continue the result will be a person that no one wants to be around. This does not have to be the case if we simply say, "you know what" I am not going to live this way; I choose to forgive those who have hurt me and not live in bitterness and resentment any longer. When you and I make the decision to do this God's Holy Spirit will come and give us the needed help to do what we cannot do otherwise. When we refuse to forgive others, whereby releasing them from bondage we are holding ourselves hostage to unforgiveness. This is dangerous in that it can lead to other sins such as having the desire to harm the person involved, damage their reputation or destroy their possessions.

Since this book is written primarily from a stand point of a follower of God and His word, it must be noted that those of you who are reading it, should consider the following: We all must make our own choices in life and if we choose the wrong path; know that there will be consequences. My choice is to let forgiveness be active in my heart and for me to experience the forgiveness of God through Jesus Christ. Freedom is then made available through the power of His name.

Finally, if we have done something that we know is wrong and suffered the consequences because we were guilty, we certainly cannot deny the fact that we deserved the sentence that was given. Even though we may have removed ourselves from under the blood of Jesus and given Satan the opportunity to work within us. The truth is if we give in to temptation; we can be assured the result of that sin is bondage. Once you are determined to seek Jesus and cry out to Him in repentance; asking Him for forgiveness and cleansing, you can be certain that you have been forgiven. There could be one thing that keeps a person from receiving forgiveness and that is not forgiving yourself. We cannot continue to beat ourselves up repeatedly, feeling that we have failed Jesus therefore not deserving His forgiveness. This is just another ploy that Satan uses.

Remember Jesus will forgive us when we confess our sin. It does not matter what sin we have committed He has cleansed us and He absolutely has no remembrance of our sins anymore. The Prophet Isaiah declares this as being true in Isaiah 43:25 KJV, "I, even I, am he that blotteth out thy transgressions for mine own sake, and will not remember thy sins." Therefore, we are not to allow the enemy to hold us in bondage. What should be our reaction to this truth? It should be one of rejoicing because we are forgiven!

Prayer: Lord God, it is you that has warned us against harboring unforgiveness in our hearts. If it was not a serious condition you would not have addressed, it as such. Help us to pay attention to our hearts and if there is just a tiny seed of unforgiveness found there please give us the needed help to rid ourselves of it, whereby the continuous forgiveness of Jesus will be granted to us. Thank you for your help in Jesus Name. Amen

Chapter 4

A Heart of Love

Love is what makes the world go around, so it has been said. There have been songs written and sang about the need for it. Dionne Warwick had a popular song back in the early sixties with the title, "What the world needs now is love". A few of the lyrics goes like this:
What the world needs now is love sweet love,
It's the only thing that there's just too little of,
What the world needs now is love sweet love,
No, not just for some but for everyone……….

     Love then is a key force and emotion that is needed by all regardless of color, culture, social status or religious affiliation. The need to be loved and cared for is so powerful until it causes a person to look for it in places that are not very favorable because of what may go on in them. How can we make people love us or what can we change about ourselves that can ignite a spark of love in a person's heart for us? For women it could be the loss of weight or to dress provocatively drawing attention to themselves. The list of things is endless which may be used to earn someone's love. Wealth or position of authority may even be used. These are extreme measures when used, but it happens and will continue to happen, sad to say.

Love is real, and a strong emotion. For it is stated that it is "stronger than death". Is this true? Yes, it is true for its a statement that comes from the Bible. Solomon penned these words in the Book, Songs of Solomon, "Set me as a seal upon thine heart, as a seal upon thine arm: for love is strong as death; jealousy is cruel as the grave: the coals thereof are coals of fire, which hath a most vehement flame" (Song of Solomon 8:6, KJV). This type of love is what is expressed between a man and a woman. In the Greek it is known as "phileo" love.

Consider if you will when two people meet and eventually they feel such a strong affection for one another until all they think about is each other. It becomes even stronger and they conclude that it's the real thing, "True Love". They take the next step and get married expecting to live happily ever after. This must be so because they really love each other, they are perfect for each other. Therefore, they are destined to be together until the end. The honeymoon was fabulous and even the little differences between them could not dampen their new life together. They rent an apartment and settle in with new furniture and appliances. Everything is working out just fine and even having to adjust to each other's habits did not present a problem. You know the usual ones for example, taking out the garbage, picking up dirty clothes, or check the toilet seat. These were just minor things that they had to work through and come to grips with. So, they endured these tests and minor scrimmages.

The big surprise came when they received news that they were expecting their first child. To say they were excited is an understatement. They began to think about getting a larger apartment because they would need more space. The discussion quickly changed to one of buying a house in a nice area and that would fit into their budget. They find the perfect house and move in and begin to fix up the nursery in anticipation of the baby's arrival. It was agreed that she would continue to work until the baby is born after which she could resign and stay home. Life seemed to be just perfect and they could not be any happier. The baby is born, and they are both learning to care for a little one as well as adjusting to new sleep patterns. He helped as much as possible the first couple of weeks, but he must return to work. This was challenging but they met it and came through this period of major adjustment. Fast forward ten years later another child has been added to the family and another house which is larger and cost more than the first one. They are doing well and are respected in the community, but things have changed in their relationship.

What is going on? There is no real warmth or open communication about how things are going with the kids. When they are together it lacks spark and passion that once was there. It is as if they are no longer connected. He spends more time with the guys especially during football season. She feels that she has the responsibility of caring for the kids, taking them to school, gymnastic or soccer practice. Plus, she has gained a few pounds, and nothing seems to fit anymore. She is feeling as though he is no longer interested in her because of the weight. Maybe it would be better if they just separate for a while or just end it by getting a quick divorce. He has moved up in the company and she feel trapped since she is not doing anything with her degree in engineering. Then there is the issue of money. How much money does she spend and what is it being spent on. This has become a big issue even to the point of arguments in front of the kids.

On the other hand, he is not happy, and it is beginning to cause him to drink a little more than normal. The questions in his head that are whirling around and around, "do you love her anymore? Will things be better if we just end it?" Or "What about the kids?" It is not the same and it's seemingly getting worse. "She just does not understand or meet my needs anymore. "I need a way out and the best way is to leave, file for divorce and start all over." He is thinking how can this possibly be happening when we really did love each other once? It is her who is wrong, for she is not submitting to me according to what the Bible declares. On the other hand, she is thinking, "How can this be happening when we really did love each other? Isn't love supposed to be forever and isn't it supposed to help solve all the problems that we may encounter? He is just being selfish, and he never thinks about my needs; isn't he supposed to do everything that he can to make me happy? I don't love him anymore; actually, I hate him for what he is doing to me!"

What happened to this couple happens to many couples who have the same mindset that they will live happily ever after because they are in love. This love is based upon human feeling and unrealistic expectations. We as humans cannot guarantee one another's happiness. It does not matter what we do it will never be good enough. We are selfish at best and we expect others to cater to our every need. When this doesn't happen, it causes our world to fall apart; and we are miserable and therefore we make others that we are close to miserable as well. To expect those that love us to jump through hoops to make sure we are fulfilled and happy is wrong and it's very selfish and prideful.

God has called us to love each other and He has provided instructions on how to accomplish it. It is only possible with His help. He offers that help through His indwelling presence. He has given us the ability to love as He loves. God spoke these words to the Apostle Paul, "For it is God which worketh in you both to will and to do of his good pleasure" (Philippians 2:13, KJV). God commands us to walk in love toward one another. This is not something that He takes lightly since God Himself is love. This is called AGAPE love in the Greek, for it is the God kind of love that is available to those who would come to Jesus and allow Him to become Lord over their lives. God's command is that first we love God with all our hearts and all of our soul, mind and strength. The second command goes along with the first, "We are to love our neighbor as ourselves". Since He is love, can He not cause His love to fill our hearts? When we learn to love God and put Him first in our lives everything else will fall into alignment with His plan, becoming easier to deal with in our everyday lives.

When a heart is filled with God's love through the power of the Holy Spirit, it does not want to get its own way. When there is a problem or a wrong that has come about it will take the necessary steps to work toward a resolution and ultimately toward forgiveness. Concerning the marriage relationship there are some very key pointers that Apostle Paul writes about in the fifth chapter of Ephesians. He tells the wife, "to submit to her own husband, as unto the Lord" (Ephesians 5:22, KJV). This Scripture is often taken out of context to make wives feel guilty if they are not doing everything that their husbands demand. God did not instruct the Apostle to write this to make wives feel inferior or to become slaves to their husbands. This has to do with headship which is not based on superiority. We know that the man Adam was created first and Eve, the woman was formed second. Yet, they were not to lord it over each other, but to be lord or master of God's creation.

Therefore, God speaks through Paul and gives counsel to men concerning wives; and to wives regarding husbands. After he tells the wife to be subject or submissive to her own husband. Listen to what he writes: "That he might sanctify and cleanse it with the washing of water by the word, that he might present it to himself a glorious church, not having spot, or wrinkle, or any such thing; but that it should be holy and without blemish. So ought men to love their wives as their own bodies. He that loveth his wife loveth himself. For no man ever yet hated his own flesh; but nourisheth and cherisheth it, even as the Lord the church: For we are members of his body, of his flesh, and of his bones. For this cause shall a man leave his father and mother, and shall be joined unto his wife, and they two shall be one flesh. This is a great mystery: but I speak concerning Christ and the church. Nevertheless, let every one of you in particular so love his wife even as himself; and the wife see that she reverence her husband" (Ephesians 5:26-33, KJV).

What we can take away from Paul's advice is that respect and love is what marriage should be established on. This comes from the concept that Christ loves His bride (His body) with this type of selfless love; and He treats her with tenderness and gives her His undivided attention to cause her to feel loved and cared for in this world. He provides everything for her that is needed to make her beautiful and completely righteous or holy in His and the Father's sight.

This is pure and selfless love that was demonstrated by God when He accepted the Son's proposal to become man and give his life on behalf of mankind. The love of God was and still is on display as it was when John wrote: " For God so loved the world, that he gave his only begotten Son, that whosoever believeth in him should not perish, but have everlasting life" (John 3:16, KJV).

God loved all of mankind even though we were all separated from Him through our sinful nature. Jesus willingly chose to give His life for us and He agreed with the Father in that He was certain that He was loved; and wanted man to be brought back into that love relationship. This was decided even though we did not love God and could not love Him because we were unable to respond to His love. The truth is that we could not love God because we did not know Him, for God is love. The Apostle John makes something else clear as well when He wrote, "Herein is love, not that we loved God, but that he loved us, and sent his Son to be the propitiation for our sins" (1 John 4:10, KJV). God loved us even when we could not love Him in return, for He knew that His love was strong enough and would never fail.

It was Jesus who prayed that we would know Gods' love in the way that He Himself had experienced the Fathers' love (John 17). Mankind in and of himself is not capable of loving God, others nor himself with genuine love because that capacity was swallowed up by the nature of Satan. His nature is complete hatred! But Jesus came to bring that love down to the world and it was sealed on the cross when He declared "it is finished". When we come to Him and surrender to His Lordship that love is born in us. How do I know that this is true, simply because He tells us that we become new creations in Christ; old things are gone and the new has come. When we are born again the capacity to love God, others and even ourselves enters our hearts (inner man, spirit).

Now! It must be allowed to work in us, that is we can choose to love with the love of God in and by Christ Jesus; or we can choose not to walk in love. It is a choice that each of us must make since Jesus will not force or coerce us into walking in His love. He will help us as soon as we admit that we have gotten off the "love path".
Meaning that we have stopped the love from flowing out of us by giving in to strife, criticism or becoming judgmental. Once we recognize that this is the case we must respond by asking Him for forgiveness and to fill our hearts with His overflowing love.

Love is strong, and it will cover a multitude of sins as Peter tells us in his letter. The love that he is referring to is God's love. For it was because of sin that Jesus went to the cross to die in our place. His love covered the sin of Adam and Eve who were disobedient to His direct command. Not only did it cover the original sin of our first parents, but every sin that all of mankind would commit. It has been said that "it was not the nails that held Jesus to the cross, but it was love". Love that is in our heart need to be allowed to come out and the best way to do that is to give it away. May be the object of that love is not deserving of it but when we think about it, neither were we deserving of the love God has given on our behalf through Christ Jesus. Even on the best of days when trying to dot every "I' or cross every "T" we still do not merit His unconditional love. But thank God that He was willing to love us anyway.

When we as followers of Christ run into trials or problems in our daily lives, we will receive the necessary strength to persevere and not give up because of what we are facing. We can have confident hope because God has assured us of salvation because of His great love for us. The Apostle Paul writes, "For when we were yet without strength, in due time Christ died for the ungodly. But God commendeth his love toward us, in that, while we were yet sinners, Christ died for us" (Romans 5:6, 8, KJV). Only someone who can love although the one for whom He had chosen to lavish his unconditional love upon is incapable of responding in the same manner. Yet, he [God] still pours out His limitless love on us. The proof is in the pudding so "they say". So, the evidence of God's love was in the death of His Son.

Critics may argue, "Yes, but that is God and He has no barriers when it comes to always responding to people in the spirit of love." He can't respond in any other way simply because He is God. Such thinking is based upon human reasoning rather than on the evidence of what Christ did for us by His death and resurrection; which is the spiritual outcome of His sacrifice. Children of God are given His Spirit to live within their hearts and are now called "sons of God". Because of His Spirit abiding in us we can love others. Sure, we must allow love to operate through us and we can do that by refusing to give in to negative spirits like, prejudice, resentment, anger, revenge or the big one which is to just simply walk in hate. This type of living does not come about over-night but is a process and a continuous desire to please the Lord by loving others as He has loved us. I strongly believe that we can get to that place because this is what God has destined for us as His children. It will come about through our growing up into His love. When we give love a place in our hearts it can't do anything other than flow outwardly.

Every member that is the true or authentic member of the body of Christ will ultimately come to that place of mature love. It is part of our destiny and it's in our DNA which is from the very fiber of Jesus Christ our Lord and Savior. We have been destined to grow up into the love of God and those who will submit to His Spirit by faith will reach that very height. For this is what He has said and is saying through His word. Paul was commissioned to get this message out to the body [the church] in his letter to the Ephesians. The third chapter of this letter makes it clear that every one of us who are born again and called out saints of God will without exception grow up in love. Paul is not just stating this, but this is his prayer for the "called out ones" of God. Listen to what he prays, "That he would grant you, according to the riches of his glory, to be strengthened with might by his Spirit in the inner man; That Christ may dwell in your hearts by faith; that ye, being rooted and grounded in love, May be able to comprehend with all saints what is the breadth, and length, and depth, and height; And to know the love of Christ, which passeth knowledge, that ye might be filled with all the fulness of God" (Ephesians 3:16-19 KJV).

When I read this repeatedly it is like getting a picture of God's great love that could be described as an ocean or a high mountain. Is it possible to understand the width, the length, the height or the depth of His love? Even if it is not possible to fully get there we must be determined to reach that goal. Paul ends his prayer for the church (past and present) with this request, "May you encounter the love of Christ, despite the fact it is too great to grasp fully". It is as if Paul is given this extra revelation and it is important for us to know. He pauses so to speak to make this point clear. He is requesting that we experience the love of God. So, we will know what it is like and that there is no doubt that it is the genuine love of God. For we have encountered His love for ourselves. It has become a reality to us and does not matter what opinions other may have. They will not be able to convince us otherwise. God's love has gone beyond the intellect and has entered our heart.

This type of love will bring us who are believers into unity. God heard Jesus pray and He answered that prayer (with "yes") as soon as it was out of Jesus' heart. "I pray that they will be one just as you and I are one – As you are in me, Father, and I am in you". But Jesus has another purpose that expands beyond the unity of His followers. To open the eyes of the unbelievers He says, "So that they may be in us so that the world will believe that you sent me" (John 17:33a). All of this is in His heart and comes out in His high priestly prayer before Father. He had given His followers the glory that His Father had given Him (the very essence of Himself). This was necessary to experience oneness with each other just as He and the Father experienced it. But there was something else that they needed to understand and experience as well. Not only they [the disciples] were or we [us as followers today] would be in perfect unity just as the Father and Jesus were, but the world would know that God the Father had sent Him [Jesus]; and that God loves them as much as God loves Me. (See John 17:33b).

    This again is I believe the very heart of Jesus and His desire for us to really understand the passionate love the Father has for us. Jesus was about to take that long walk up to the Cross of Calvary and He took the time to pray not only for the disciples then but those who would come after them. He concludes this prayer request by asking that the ones the "Father had given Him would be where I am" (kept hidden in His presence). Why did He want them to be with Him? The answer is given to us when He says, "Father, I will that they also, whom thou hast given me, be with me where I am; that they may behold my glory, which thou hast given me: for thou lovedst me before the foundation of the world" (John 17:24, KJV).

    The disciples had not experienced all of Christ's glory up to that point in that He had laid it aside to live in a human body. Once resurrected from the dead He would again take up that same glory that He had before the foundation of the world began. All of this has to do with the depth of the love of God for His Son and those who would be loved by Him. Can't you see this wonderful picture displayed before us?

    This love is not passive or limited and it is simply a force that is real proceeding from the heart of Him who is love, God! Those of us who are part of His family through faith in His Son Jesus will be brought into complete unity before we behold Him face to face. I believe that before the church is taken out of this world the evidence that we are genuine children of God will be manifested. How will it be seen? Jesus Himself provided the answer when He made the statement to the disciples the night of the Passover meal. Jesus is about to be taken from them and treated as an impostor and a criminal.

Yet, He was not concerned about what is about to happen to Himself, but He feels the sorrow of their hearts over His leaving them. So, He speaks to them by saying, "Little children, (they are precious and dear to Him), yet a little while I am with you. Ye shall seek me: and as I said unto the Jews, Whither I go, ye cannot come; so now I say to you." He goes on to say, "A new commandment I give unto you, that ye love one another; as I have loved you, that ye also love one another.". And He gives them the reason behind this new commandment when He says, "By this shall all men know that ye are my disciples, if ye have love one to another" (John 13:33-35, KJV).

God's love is in us because we have been reborn through the life of His Righteous Son, Jesus Christ. The question is, will we allow it to operate in us and through us? We should consider the love that Jesus demonstrated for us when He chose death on the cross. Oh! What love of which you and I are so undeserving. If we really know this about ourselves, then we should willingly want to give it to others of whom we know are unlovable and unworthy as well.

Paul devotes a full chapter about this love in the thirteenth chapter of 1 Corinthians. Most of us have read this passage of Scripture and or heard it read numerous of times. Listen to what Paul writes: "Though I speak with the tongues of men and of angels, and have not charity, I am become as sounding brass, or a tinkling cymbal. And though I have the gift of prophecy, and understand all mysteries, and all knowledge; and though I have all faith, so that I could remove mountains, and have not charity, I am nothing. And though I bestow all my goods to feed the poor, and though I give my body to be burned, and have not charity, it profiteth me nothing. Charity suffereth long, and is kind; charity envieth not; charity vaunteth not itself, is not puffed up, Doth not behave itself unseemly, seeketh not her own, is not easily provoked, thinketh no evil; Rejoiceth not in iniquity, but rejoiceth in the truth; Beareth all things, believeth all things, hopeth all things, endureth all things. Charity never faileth: but whether there be prophecies, they shall fail; whether there be tongues, they shall cease; whether there be knowledge, it shall vanish away. For we know in part, and we prophesy in part. But when that which is perfect is come, then that which is in part shall be done away. When I was a child, I spake as a child, I understood as a child, I thought as a child: but when I became a man, I put away childish things. For now we see through a glass, darkly; but then face to face: now I know in part; but then shall I know even as also I am known. And now abideth faith, hope, charity, these three; but the greatest of these is charity" (1 Corinthians 13:1-13, KJV).

How marvelous is this picture of love! Love is the most powerful working of God toward all of mankind. It is what makes faith work or effective (See Galatians 5:6). When all the children of God grow up into this love then the church would have reached its maturity. This is what must take place in each individual person who is called by the name of the Lord Jesus Christ. How then can we know this truth? It is simply because it is written in the word of God. Paul admonished the church at Ephesus as well as the church of today to live worthy of the vocation [lifestyle] of which they had been called. He tells them to live what was becoming to them, a life of complete lowliness of mind (humble attitude of mind) and meekness (being kind and gentle and unselfish) with long-suffering (putting up with or being patient with each other), in love. This was the key ingredient that would bring about the expected result. For which they were to, "Endeavour to keep the unity (oneness) of the Spirit in the bond of peace" (Ephesians 4:1-3).

We are to be eager for and go after this unity with all that is within us. Nevertheless, the church is going to be successful in this quest because Jesus is going to make sure that it happens. Love is the governing factor or glue that will cause every one of us to be joined together in perfect unity. No one will be disconnected from the whole body. All will be connected and fused together permanently by the Spirit of love. In conclusion! God is love and His love will never fail for it is for all eternity. "Beloved, let us love one another: for love is of God; and everyone that loveth is born of God, and knoweth God. Herein is love, not that we loved God, but that he loved us, and sent his Son to be the propitiation for our sins" (1 John 4:7,10, KJV).

Prayer: Father, you alone are perfect love and you revealed your love to us through Jesus coming to die in our place. We are not deserving of your love and never will be. There is nothing that we can give to you for choosing to love us unconditionally. All we can offer to you is a heart that is filled with thankfulness and a desire to love You; so that your love will flow out of us to others. Continually pour your love out into our hearts that we can love as You love. Thank you for your amazing love. In Jesus name! Amen.

Chapter 5

The Perfect Heart

Now! We have come to the final condition that must take place in us as we pursue the heart of God. All those things that have been discussed in the previous chapters bring us to this last stage of our quest. This quest is none other than to have reached the place of perfection. The perfect heart is a heart that is covered by Jesus and all that God the Father sees is His reflection. Everything that has once dominated the inner man has been replaced by a new creation. He has taken away the hard, selfish and rebellious heart and transformed it into a heart that is alive and flowing with His very life. Darkness that once hid the light is not able to overtake the very illumination of His presence.

I for one have longed for this to take place in my life. It would be safe to say that there are others who feel and desire this as well. Paul the great Apostle desired it to the point that he said, "Not as though I had already attained, either were already perfect: but I follow after if that I may apprehend that for which also I am apprehended of Christ Jesus. Brethren, I count not myself to have apprehended: but *this* one thing *I do*, forgetting those things which are behind, and reaching forth unto those things which are before" (Philippians 3:12-13, KJV). Yet, a few years later he could write to Timothy and say, "I have finished my course, I have fought a good fight; henceforth is laid up for me a crown of righteousness that shall be given to me; and not to me only but to everyone who love His appearing" (2 Timothy 4:7-8, KJV).

Personally, I believe that Paul had reached that place of completion in Christ Jesus and he had to be transferred from this earth because of it. This place is reserved for all of those who are children of God through their relationship with Jesus. Paul wrote about this in Ephesians chapter four and all had to do with being filled completely with the "Holy Love of God". Paul writes here in this passage these words: "He that descended is the same also that ascended up far above all heavens, that he might fill all things.) And he gave some, apostles; and some, prophets; and some, evangelists; and some, pastors and teachers; For the perfecting of the saints, for the work of the ministry, for the edifying of the body of Christ: Till we all come in the unity of the faith, and of the knowledge of the Son of God, unto a perfect man, unto the measure of the stature of the fulness of Christ: That we *henceforth* be no more children, tossed to and fro, and carried about with every wind of doctrine, by the sleight of men, *and* cunning craftiness, whereby they lie in wait to deceive" (Ephesians 4:10-16, KJV).

Everything that Jesus gave to His church was to remain in place until all things were accomplished in its time frame. All things must be complete or perfected before the church will become His mature beautiful bride. Every person who is under His lordship and covering of His blood will be brought into this place of maturity. Again, this is destined to take place regardless of how things may appear in this age. There is absolutely nothing (human or spirit) that will hinder this process from occurring. I have determined to reach that place by growing in His love through the truth (God's word), faith, and obedience to Him. God desires us to reach this perfect place more than we do ourselves. He is working to bring that about in our very being. If we are serious about being with Him and reigning with Him [Jesus] throughout eternity, then we are going to have to cooperate with Him; trust Him and stay close to Him. This is a very serious matter in that it has to do with eternity. It is not to be taken lightly or the attitude of well, "As long as I do just enough to make it" things will be okay. This is not a game where you take a chance on winning; but this is going after what will last forever, and ever and ever ……. It has no ending.

Those of us who are part of the "Bride of Christ", the church will grow up into the fullness of Christ; and this should be the motivational factor surrounding our everyday lives. Jesus will help us and give us more power to keep moving forward to reach that goal. Yes, we are still in this world and live in these mortal bodies; and we are confronted by those who do not believe. We encounter spiritual adversaries that want to sabotage our walk with the Lord. Yet, we must know that we are not abandoned nor without help for He is with us and therefore the opposition we are faced with can and will not cause us to be over taken. For the Greater One, Jesus Christ is in us and therefore we can and will stand.

The work that God has begun in us on the day we were declared His offspring through the name of Jesus is being watched over carefully. I may be weak and there are times when in that weakness I fail Him, but when my heart cries out for help and forgiveness He does not reject me. He reaches out His merciful hand and gives me the grace and mercy that is needed at that time. We don't have to stay in that place of weakness. When we appeal to our faithful High Priest, Jesus the Anointed One of God for Help He will not turn us away.

Even though as weak and helpless human beings we have access to His strength. He has the authority to work in us and fill us with His mighty power while we are yet in these earthly bodies. If our focus is on how imperfect and weak we are, this will be the image that is going to dominate our lives. God is perfect, and He tells us that this is the case, but He then pronounced or commanded, "You be perfect as your Father is perfect". This is the image that we should keep before our eyes and the confession that should come out of our mouths as well. This should be the confession of all born again believers in Christ, "I am perfect in Christ". If it sounds strange to the ear or hard to grasp then continue to say it, "I am perfect in Christ".

This confession is not a delusion, it is the way the Father sees us. Since He knows that about us, we should agree with His assessment. Perfection is simply becoming all that God is in His holiness. Yes, that is what His righteousness leads us into, and we have been declared the righteousness of God in Christ Jesus. It is not of ourselves, but it has been granted or deposited into us through the life of Jesus through faith.

Therefore, as we align our lives with His will and purpose through faith, and total dependency on Him He will see to it that we reach that higher place He has set for us. This is the destiny of the Bride of Christ and its truth cannot be over emphasized. Can it be that this is what Jesus and the Father have longed for throughout eternity? God spoke by the Holy Spirit to Paul and made it clear that He would make sure this takes place when Paul writes, "Being confident of this very thing, that he which hath begun a good work in you will perform it until the day of Jesus Christ" (Philippians 1:6, KJV). This is something that we can be confident about and consider it to be already complete as God Himself does; and we will not be made ashamed because it is from God and by God.

      The Apostle John got a picture of what the Apostle Paul said would happen to Christ's church as stated in Ephesians, "He makes the whole body fit together perfectly. As each part does its own special work, it helps the other parts grow, so that the whole body is healthy and growing and full of love" (Ephesians 4:16 KJV). This is what I believe John the Beloved Apostle could see when he was abandoned on the Isle of Patmos. This is what was revealed to John: And from the throne came a voice that said, "And a voice came out of the throne, saying, Praise our God, all ye his servants, and ye that fear him, both small and great. And I heard as it were the voice of a great multitude, and as the voice of many waters, and as the voice of mighty thunderings, saying, Alleluia: for the Lord God omnipotent reigneth. Let us be glad and rejoice, and give honour to him: for the marriage of the Lamb is come, and his wife hath made herself ready.   And to her was granted that she should be arrayed in fine linen, clean and white: for the fine linen is the righteousness of saints" (Revelation 19:5-8, KJV).

      This is the living church of God purchased by the blood of His Dear Son. These are made up of living stones that are you and me who know Him and are walking and living as His true called out ones now in this world. This is not a fantasy, but it is real. It is supernatural and therefore it is spiritual and must be received by faith. In the Book of Hebrews there is a passage that describes the faithful ones who have gone before us, and the writer has placed a little nugget right before us which talks about the church and those who were declared righteous before God. And here is what he wrote, "But ye are come unto mount Sion, and unto the city of the living God, the heavenly Jerusalem, and to an innumerable company of angels" (Hebrews 12:22 KJV).

This is what Jesus saw from the foundation of the world. He is waiting for all things to be complete in this present age. When God determines that everything is ready, He will declare the Wedding Day of the Son of His Love and His Bride, the Church (See Revelation 19:7-8). He will come and take her to Himself for the consummation of all things have come. A glorious celebration will then take place. I believe that it is what Jude declares will happen to us and because Jesus has kept us for this very moment of time. Jude writes: "Now unto him that is able to keep you from falling, and to present *you* faultless before the presence of his glory with exceeding joy" (Jude 1:24, KJV).

What a glorious time this is going to be and I for one want to be in on this and have made the decision that I will be there. This is a goal that is set before all of us who have put our trust in Jesus. He is the one who will guard us and help us get to this place of completion. It is through His ministry and life that God will bring us into the fullness of the stature of His Dear Son. This is perfection, which means that we are completely "Holiness" unto Him. Therefore, we will live with Him forever. That sounds like eternity does it not? This is God's plan and He is the one who is watching over it to bring it to an expected end. So, I choose to believe what He has done and is about to do. Let the "Redeemed of the Lord say so, I am complete in Christ."

In 1999 the contemporary Christian group, Parachute Band released the song "Complete In You". It is a powerful worship song that I believe speaks to this very subject.

Lyrics:

Here I am, Oh God
I bring this sacrifice
My open heart, I offer up my life
I look to You, Lord
Your love that never ends
Restores me again
So I lift my eyes to you Lord
In your strength will I break through Lord
Touch me now, let your love fall down on me
I know your love dispels all my fears
Through the storm I will hold on Lord

And by faith I will walk on Lord
Then I'll see beyond my Calvary one day
And I will be complete in You

Here I am, Oh God
I bring this sacrifice
My open heart, I offer up my life
I look to You, Lord
Your love that never ends
Restores me again

So I lift my eyes to you Lord
In your strength will I break through Lord
Touch me now, let your love fall down on me
I know your love dispels all my fears
Through the storm I will hold on Lord
And by faith I will walk on Lord
Then I'll see beyond my Calvary one day
And I will be complete in You

I look to You, Lord
Your love that never ends
Restores me again

So I lift my eyes to you Lord
In your strength will I break through Lord
Touch me now, let your love fall down on me
I know your love dispels all my fears
Through the storm I will hold on Lord
And by faith I will walk on Lord

Then I'll see beyond my Calvary one day
And I will be complete in
I will be complete in
I will be complete in You

Prayer: Holy Father, you are glorious and righteous altogether. Lord you are beautiful and clean, and your holiness is your attribute. Yet, through the righteous one, Jesus we have access to your holiness. Develop that nature in us so that we will come into that place of completion and perfection in yourself. You are making us into the very likeness and image of your Son; and therefore, this requires us to be holy. So, bring this about Lord God, for the glory of Your Son and for the good of all those who are Your children. In Jesus Name I ask this and thank you for it. Amen!

About the Author

Charlene Gray was born and raised in Arkansas. She was called to preach and teach the Word of God in the early eighties. She is a licensed minster with the primary focus on teaching the uncompromising truth of God's Word. There is a tremendous desire within her for the study of the Bible and a passion to see believers discover their passion for the Word and by living it out in their daily lives. She has been active in the Jonesboro, Arkansas Church of God of Prophecy for over twenty years; and is a member of the State's Women Ministry Team assisting the director in ministry during ladies' retreats. Charlene is married and has three adult sons, two of which are married, and are parents to her two grandsons and two grand-daughters.

For more information, contact Charlene at:

chargray10@yahoo.com

Made in the USA
Lexington, KY
07 December 2019